Published by Beadle Books

New York and London

2024

Copyright © 2024 Yunus Tuncel

Book Design: Seth Binsted

ISBN: 978-0-9962058-5-6 (Paperback)

ISBN: 979-8-3481-3889-9 (Ebook)

Notebook E: Eroticism
And the Devil Gave the Poison to Eros

Eroticians of the world, unite! It is high time to fuck the world!

Erotic Observations from 2018 to 2023

Yunus Tuncel

New York

Contents

Preface 11
Preliminary Insights 14
The Erotic Selfhood 19
Erotica and the Senses 22
Psycho-Somatic Forces 24
Eroticism and the Stages of Life 26
Erotic Gods: Eroticism and Religion 28
Erotic Activities and Transgression 32
Eros and Hades: Where Death Sets its Limits 35
Is Eroticism Uniquely Human? The Human, the Animal
and the Non-human in Eroticism 36
Emotions 38
Askesis 41
Arts 43
On the "Transcendental" Conditions of Erotic Experience ... 44
Schools of Philosophy and Eroticism 46
Environment and the Objects of the World 48
Eros and Power 50
Antithetical to Eroticism 53
Eroticism in the Age of Posthumanism 56
How the World of Eros Finally Fell into Oblivion in the West .. 58
World Erotica and the Historic Context 61
Reflections on the Eroticians of the World 67
Epilogue 76

Acknowledgements

I would like to thank two important people who made this book possible: David Kilpatrick for making his publishing joint, Beadle Press, available and Seth Binsted for designing the book.

To think a thing evil means to make it evil. The passions become evil and malicious if they are regarded as evil and malicious. Thus Christianity has succeeded in transforming Eros and Aphrodite – great powers capable of idealisation – into diabolical kobolds and phantoms by means of the torments it introduces into the consciences of believers whenever they are excited sexually. Is it not dreadful to make necessary and regularly recurring sensations into a source of inner misery, and in this way to want to make inner misery a necessary and regularly recurring phenomenon in every human being! In addition to which it remains a misery kept secret and thus more deeply rooted: for not everyone possesses the courage of Shakespeare to confess his Christian gloominess on this point in the way he did in his Sonnets. — Must everything that one has to combat, that one has to keep within bounds or on occasion banish totally from one's mind, always have to be called evil! Is it not the way of common souls always to think an enemy must be evil! And ought one to call Eros an enemy? The sexual sensations have this in common with the sensations of sympathy and worship, that one person, by doing what pleases him, gives pleasure to another person — such benevolent arrangements are not to be found so very often in nature! And to culminate such an arrangement and to ruin it through associating it with a bad conscience! — In the end this diabolising of Eros acquired an outcome in comedy: thanks to the dark secretiveness of the church in all things erotic, the 'devil' Eros gradually became more interesting to mankind than all the saints and angels put together: the effect has been that, to this very day, the love story is the only thing which all circles find equally interesting — and with an exaggeratedness which antiquity would have found incomprehensible, and which will one day again elicit laughter. All out thinking and poetising, from the highest to the lowest, is characterised, and more than characterised, by the excessive importance attached to the love story: on this account it may be that posterity will judge the whole inheritance of Christian culture to be marked by something crack-brained and petty.

~ Nietzsche, Daybreak, 76

Preface

1

Eros has his own signs, signals, and signification.

2

In Eros we trust: this would be the revolution for humanity.

3

Eroticians! Be aware and wary of moralists! They will be your doom and gloom!

4

Eroticism assumes a healthy culture and practice of sexuality.

5

Eroticism is the explosion of libido in an unusual and extraordinary setting.

6

Erotic activity shatters the everyday world, as the heterogeneous penetrates into the homogeneous.

7

The reason why one forgets to be erotic is similar to why adults forget how to be playful. This, however, constitutes a paradox for human existence, a riddle for the adventurer to solve.

8

The child is playful, but typically not sexually active, at least not in the way adults are; on the other hand, the adults is expected to be sexually active and yet has stopped being playful. To be erotic one needs to take the sexual adult back to the child and recover playfulness in the field of libidinous energies.

9

Modern pornography is the end of playfulness; it pretends to be heterogeneous, but, to a large extent, belongs to the homogeneous order. There is nothing scandalous in contemporary porno.

10

The time of erotic activity is cyclical; this is to say, in it the forces of life and death meet each other head on. In it, both lovers are active and passive in roughly equal measures, even when one side's action meets the other side's inaction. This, however, can not be a perpetual state, as the roles change. In other words, in eroticism no participant is fully passive, but is rather a creative participant in the erotic action.

Preliminary Insights

11

Eroticism is for the few; what the many do is ordinary sex, mostly for pleasure and procreation.

12

Erotic experience is rare and the scope of this rarity stems from the society in which one lives.

13

In the erotic activity, the forces concupiscence concur.

14

A healthy sexual life is a necessity for eroticism.

15

Players in the field of eroticism are on similar emotive planes.

16

Eroticism is not teleological; there is no purpose to erotic activities. It is rather a process.

17

Contra telos in eros. Eroticism is not only a matter of pricks and holes but also, and more importantly, erotic signification and communion.

18

In the erotic bond there is a conflux of the ordinary and the extraordinary.

19

In eroticism, drives that are typically dormant in everyday life get activated.

20

One has to form and re-form the sex drive, which becomes ludic in the erotic act.

21

The aggressive charge of the death drive in sex becomes meaningful when it is reciprocal.

22

Physical violence, even if it is reciprocal, is not a *sine qua non* of the erotic experience.

23

Eroticism is the refined and reoriented sublimation of the sex drive and it is a holistic experience.

24

Expediency and utility cheapen the erotic experience.

25

In eroticism, fantasy and reality meet.

26

In an erotic act, the bubble of everyday life is pricked, which bursts into a flow of libidinal energy.

27

Eroticism assumes leisure, or else, it is just simple sexual activity. It is through otium that the sexual attraction, bond, and activity become free.

28

Eroticism flourishes where there is leisure and a class of those who pursue leisurely activities. It is the surplus of human activity, beyond the activity of everydayness and self-preservation.

29

Eroticism demands subtlety, refinement, spontaneity and a rich imagination.

30

Physical or mental disability does not constitute a hindrance to erotic experience.

31

There is no mystery to sexuality in itself, mystery lies in eroticism, the field of spontaneity, discretion, creativity and transgression!

32

Eroticism is almost always transgressive, whether it is in closed traditional or open liberal societies. The nature of transgression changes from one to the next.

33

Not every deviation from procreative sex must be considered to be erotic; deviation, however, is essential to any erotic deed.

34

Richness of the milieu and objects found there enhance eroticism and provide new and diverse stimulants for the erotic practitioner. Attraction to diversity must be approached not only from the angle of newness but also that of abundance. After all, life is bountiful, and eroticism is its fullest expression.

The Erotic Selfhood

35

An erotic self is self-exciting and would not suffer from passive boredom.

36

An overall *askesis* for the care of the self must include erotic formation, as in many ancient practices.

37

A rich soul can sustain different forms of love in one's self, friendly love, family love, universal love and erotic love, without letting one of them gain the upper hand, as it happened in the Middle Ages with the victory of Agape over Eros. Ultimately, all are needed for the vitality of individual and cultural life.

38

The primary modes of operation and relation in eroticism lie in the predisposition of partners in an erotic encounter. Consent, dictated by law and society, is a construct of consciousness, whereas the 'proper' disposition is a function of unconsciousness.

39

One must be a cultivated human being to have the 'proper' erotic disposition so that one 'knows' when, where and how to enter into the erotic space, an erotic experience with the other who is similarly disposed.

40

Eroticism is not about consensus but rather concurrence. While the former happens at the level of consciousness, the latter that of pre- and un-consciousness, as signification prior to consciousness.

41

Since human life and society are diverse and ultimately humans are singular beings, there cannot be one recipe for erotic experiences for everyone. One must be creative in one's own context and circumstances.

42

Fantasy and erotica. Erotic life starts with a fantasy; not every fantasy though can be actualized. However, some fantasies need to be externalized –less withholding turns the soul into a den of frustration– so as to give life to them. In the actualization of the fantasy, when it involves others, the main criteria are who the partners are and the reciprocal affectivity on all participants in making the fantasy come to life.

40

Recent archaeological excavations and anthropological studies have presented many tools and discoveries on how ancient societies practiced their version of "ars erotica." Educators can benefit from them and promote sex and erotic education for youth so that they find their own erotic selves. Finally, laws must not hinder such erotic formation.

Erotica and the Senses

44

Sticky and stinky: erotica happens in dark matter.

45

In the erotic act, senses open up to wider horizon.

46

Senses mingle with each other as in synesthesia.

47

The wings of desire moan with pain and pleasure.

45

In the erotic act, senses open up to wider horizon.

46

Senses mingle with each other as in synesthesia.

47

The wings of desire moan with pain and pleasure.

48

One sees, hears, smells and tastes through limbs.

49

All body parts can be eroticized in their right time and place.

50

In eroticism all senses and sense-perceptions are sexualized, as the gaze, the touch, the smell, the sight, and the taste blend in an orgiastic communion.

51

The eroticist understands the different, complex functions of the senses, including those that are not sexual, and acts erotically in the ripe moment and situation.

Psycho-Somatic Forces

52

Movement, fitness, agility and mobility are essential to erotic practices.

53

Exhaustion of the body does not erase or efface the erotic desire; it only retards its physical manifestation since physical energies are finite. What is at crux is not this type of exhaustion but rather cultural lethargy that keeps all energies in a stasis of complacency.

54

All bodily regimes that are cultivated and practiced in societies, such as sex, sport and dance, hold movement as sacred and special and explore and experience it in their own ways.

55

Dreams reveal a plethora of desirous relations and activities that one is not wont to imagine in wakeful state.

56

In the erotic act, senses open up to wider horizon.

57

Senses mingle with each other as in synesthesia.

Eroticism and the Stages of Life

58

Papasilenus is always awake and ready for sex.

59

One can be erotic in any stage of life; every stage, however, has its own needs and energy levels, consequently, its own erotic economy and practice.

60

The danger of becoming grave. The innocence of the ludic must be kept alive in the transition from childhood to adulthood; one area of the ludic is erotica. Sports, games, arts, acting, dancing, and theater share this common ground with eroticism.

61

Contra moralists! Sexual and erotic formation of children and youth must be protected the way Artemis protected her virgins and Hermes young athletes; however, such protection does not hinder that erotic formation. On the contrary, it promotes and gives it a sacred domain. Artemis, Hermes and Eros work in unison.

62

As in life, there is entry into and exit from erotic activity. It is proven to be wrong by psychoanalysis and sexology that children are asexual beings. They are on the way to sexual practice and, as such, must be educated and initiated into sexual rites, which also prepare them for eroticism. On the other hand, there must be rituals for and a noble way of exiting from sexual and erotic practices, when one is no longer able to perform them or when one has run out of libidinal energies.

Erotic Gods: Eroticism and Religion

63

When gods have sex, that is erotic.

64

Since there is only one god in monotheistic religions, the only sex left to that god is onanism. This could explain the sexual and erotic poverty in the communities that follow these religions.

65

Dionysos approaches Eros through satyrs and maenads who are the relay points to *sextasy*.

66

The sexual violence that Greek gods committed must have had an accentuation impact on the sex drive.

67

In ancient times, cult domains set the frame, the limits, and also the "freedom" for all rituals, including those of sexual nature.

68

Hinduism, though austere in ascetic practices that are harsh on the body in some realms, did, at the same time, promote erotic *askesis*, as *Kama Sutra*, among other works, testifies. This is consistent with the immanentist aspect of Hinduism, where there is a close reflective bond between mortals and gods. There are only degrees of separation between the two realms. To put in the context of eroticism, gods are sexual analogous to mortals.

69

Buddhism, on the other hand, moderated the sexual desire for the sake of diminishing human suffering. With this it took away the joy of sexual and erotic desire in at least in its mainstream form.

70

In ancient times initiation rites took place under the auspices of gods monitored by priests. Since ascetic practices were variegated and cults modulated allocation of priests and cult members according to their nature, one could expect less abuse of the novice to happen in such a system.

71

In ancient Greek culture, libidinal energies flew in a circular way in different artistic media: In drama satyrs were the erotic figures and symbols, and comedies presented lewd scenes. Vase paintings portrayed a variety of sex scenes. Lyric poetry, especially those of Sappho and Theognis, spoke of personal homoerotic love. Ancient Greek art provides a glimpse into this circuit of 'ars erotica' of their times.

72

Old vs. New Religions. Ancient religions cultivated eroticism and initiated youth into its practices. Monotheistic religions reversed this tradition, as it utterly rejected all eroticism while sullying bodily functions. Here the new is a regression, not a progression.

73

Contra mystics but for unio mystica sexualis! — In the erotic bond, one becomes unified with all beings. To deny sexuality and erotic functions goes against this basic tenet of originary mysticism. Thus block the later mystics the path to higher realms of unity.

74

The decline of libidinal economies often occur in tandem with the denial of the body and physiological functions; the "ascetic idealism" of religions obtunds the senses and sensory/sensual experiences.

Erotic Activities and Transgression

75

Transgressions, including those in the sphere of sexuality including perverted deviations from the mainstream, make humans who they are as singular beings. In one's transgressive acts, however, one must heed the voice of Moira and not be unjust towards others.

76

Erotic acts are almost always transgressive in relation to existing laws of the land, social norms or religious codes.

77

Laws and rules cannot be the sole remedy for sexual abuses; more often than not laws create problems, as they establish arbitrary rules that become repressive and restrictive.

78

In the erotic act, time and space move towards each other, where they co-mingle, as in a dark hole.

79

In the erotic act, time and space move towards each other, where they co-mingle, as in a dark hole.

80

Erotic desires and designs remain hidden and not externalized most of the time for a variety of reasons: lack of courage and fear of repercussions; possibility of being shamed and excluded from "good" society; ultimately, the fear of death. In many closed societies, the expression of some of forms of sexual desire, even if it is not unjust from a larger scheme of things, remains forbidden and criminalized.

Eros and Hades: Where Death Sets its Limits

81

Death is the end of all erotic activity and yet it is death, or rather the pending death, that instigates it. In eroticism, as a form of this-worldly transcendence, one loses oneself in the other, while death is the final loss of the self.

82

Bataille on Eros and Death. In the erotization of the dead, life turns upon itself and considers its end. This is where the pain of mortality encounters the joy of sex.

83

One dies a new death in throwing one's self onto an erotic activity that is transgressive. The new death may entail loss, even the loss of honor.

84

The soldier and the whore have one thing in common: they are not afraid of dying.

Is Eroticism Uniquely Human? The Human, the Animal and the Non-human in Eroticism

85

Fantasies of sex with animals fuel the erotic drive. Although many humans may have such desires, it is best for them to remain un-practiced, because humans cannot decode animal's erotic signification.

86

Whether eroticism belongs strictly to the human realm is not possible to attest from the stand point of non-humans.

87

From the human standpoint. Eroticism distinguishes humans from the animal world and yet one rediscovers one's animality in the erotic act.

88

In the erotic activity the beast in the human comes back to life; this could be why all accessories, real or symbolic, like leathers and feathers that come from animal life excite the partners in the act and enhance their beastly qualities.

89

Eroticism is the sublimation and transfiguration of the animal human's sexual life. Insofar as one can separate the human animal from the animal human, eroticism is a human activity; that is to say, it happens in the space of values created by humans, values placed on sexuality and sexual functions. Although it is hard to take the animal out of the human, the following criteria can be established to pursue this question: 1) eroticism is not dictated by procreation; 2) eroticism assumes that there are taboos on sexuality and these taboos are broken in the erotic act.

Emotions

90

Erotic activities have their own emotional affectivity.

91

Erotic encounters are not degrading but rather elevating.

92

If one feels *guilty*, one is not ready for the erotic adventure.

93

Pain and suffering are embedded in erotic experiences; the pain inflicted depends on the practitioner's level of tolerance. Pain and pleasure are not mutually exclusive in the erotic bond. Both Sadism and Masochism have received, and would receive, negative connotation, because of their misuse out of context. One does not inflict pain on someone else arbitrarily, but rather within the context of erotic excitement and elevation.

94

Eroticism and romantic love are not the same, although they

are not mutually exclusive. The same can be said of marriage and any other type of intimate human relation. This opens up the door for reflection on how erotic love relates to other forms of love.

95

From a phenomenological standpoint, each form of love is unique and has its own functionality and vitality. One may perfect one's self in one form but not in others, or one may lack other forms of love and not experience them at all.

96

If a culture denies and represses physical forms of love, it leaves behind a carcass of love, devoid of its visceral vibrancy. This is why it is necessary to move beyond any dualistic conception of the physical and the spiritual and arrive at a holistic approach.

97

Erotic relations can heal many problem emotions the way any healthy human relation would. At the primal level of the affects of eroticism lie creativity and ecstasy, which have healing powers. On the other hand, eroticism modulates such emotions as empathy, pain, communal joy and pleasure, and reciprocal empowerment.

Askesis

98

One must experiment on oneself to discover one's erotic self.

99

Auto-sex is the meditative posture for the erotician but it is neither the A nor the Z of erotic experience.

100

One must experiment on erotic fantasies with like-spirited eroticians.

101

It is not necessary and advisable to fulfill every erotic fantasy; one must consider the 'affect' of its fulfilment. This exceeds the discussion on consequences of actions. Erotic world thrives with a different *modus operandi* and there are different 'consequences' at best not commensurate with ordinary understanding of consequences. For instance, there is no guilt in the erotic act.

Arts

102

What form of art within the spectrum from the visual to the musical, is the most erotically stimulating depends on the individual and culture and their approach and estimation of specific forms of art.

103

One can replicate, through symbolic gestures, erotic activity in words, sounds, images and thoughts; one would thereby have erotic poetry, music, visual arts, and philosophy.

104

Modern society is accustomed to experiencing erotic art mostly textually and visually, but not musically. We have erotic novels, stories, movies, plays, etc., but where is erotic music? How would erotic music sound, especially symbolically and figuratively, if not directly and literally, and independent of their accompanying erotic imagery, as one finds it in erotic movies, for instance?

On the "Transcendental" Conditions of Erotic Experience

105

Kantians, be aware! These are the 'a priori' conditions for the transcendental unity of erotic apperception.

106

Erotic ambience sets the stage and the context for erotic encounters; it can be in private or public space.

107

Objects constitute anchorage points or cathexis relays through which erotic élan flows. These objects can be regalia or artifacts made specifically for erotic activities.

108

Both the ambience and the objects bring the erotic partners into a fold of desire, a framework where they can enter into an erotic relationship.

109

In this fold, erotic partners find entry points into each other's erotic lives so as to conjoin their inner experiences or establish bridges between them,

110

Fulfilling an erotic encounter.

111

And Hegelians, take note! Eroticism does not move upward spirally. It revolves around itself eternally.

Schools of Philosophy and Eroticism

112

Idealists, depending on their brand, would be satisfied with the idea and the ideal of sex and forego its actual practice.

113

Materialists can be caught up in the mechanics of sex if they believe in a mechanical universe.

114

Stoics deny all pleasure and all the juices and lubricants for a vibrant sex life; where there is no pleasure, eroticism would be as dry as a desert.

115

In order to be consistent, pessimists cannot engage in any sexual activity. If they did, they would be taking an active role in the "wretched world." One cannot imagine a Pascal in bed!!!

116

Fatalists would accept whatever sexual position is given to them, which they would consider God-given.

117

For nihilists, anything goes... They may open the door wider for erotic experiences but narrow the field of the spirit.

118

Stoicism and Buddhism deny pleasures and pleasure-seeking, because they believe that pleasures disturb moderation, tranquility and ultimately the path to enlightenment and Nirvana. However, with their denial of pleasure they neglect the concupiscent aspect of human life and ignore the difficult task of spiritualizing desire. Humans are desirous beings and what is needed is to bring 'spirituality' to desire and its expression, not its denial and repression.

119

Consequently, none of these schools would be conducive to and fertile grounds for erotic culture and experience.

Environment and the Objects of the World

120

When the objects of everyday life are used in erotic sex, they are imbued with a different symbolism. A stick is no longer a stick, a lily is no longer a lily, for instance.

121

Objects used and consumed in the erotic act should enhance the experience and not obtund it.

122

One must experiment with objects, along with those of one's partner, to find one's own erotic mood and temperament.

123

Intoxicants can facilitate the erotic experience and open it up to new horizons, but they are not indispensable for the erotic bond.

124

Climate, dietary regimes, ethnic and national taste and sentiments, gender constructs, norms and customs play a role in the formation of sexual desire and consequently erotic experiences.

125

New technologies can contribute to the enhancement of the erotic experience; however, erotic techniques, used for centuries from humiliation and interrogation to mummification, flogger, fisting, and golden showers cannot be replaced by new technologies. They remain erotic at primordial levels with or without the use of technology.

126

Erotic acts can take place in private, semi-private, and public realms in different levels and forms of discretion. Each realm may have its own transgressions under the norms of the society and its codes and morals.

127

One does not need material wealth to have erotic experiences, contrary to common opinions about ancient erotic practices where the leisurely class could "afford" them. Erotica is a matter of disposition, a way of sexual being-in-the-world. Most ancient arts and texts do not portray the lives of poor classes, which does not prove that they did not experience 'ars erotica.'

Eros and Power

128

Erotic power is sovereign power. In an erotic encounter, sovereign participants come together analogous to contest games.

129

A free milieu is a necessary condition for erotic activity; here 'freedom' is meant in an individual, existential sense, not in the political sense.

130

Power can excite positively or disturb negatively the erotic relations. It becomes exciting and enhancing when erotic partners in vertical power relations are in a similar plain of interest and on a parallel course of development. Otherwise, it can be one-sided, disturbing, and abusive with effects of repression on the lower end of the hierarchy.

131

Most do not know how to act *positively* when they have power over others, because they do not have power over themselves. One must be attuned to the care and exercise of power.

132

The absence of rich sexual experiences leads many to impoverished, abusive sexual relations. The libidinal energies flow the way rivers do; they must be channeled and find their proper outlets.

133

Erotic activity assumes more or less equal powers; it often operates in a field of lateral power relations. There are, however, vertical erotic relations as well. The Greek homoerotica, for example, functioned in vertical power relations because it was geared towards the education of youth. The erotica of troubadours and trobairitz also assumed vertical power relations based on medieval/feudal models, as the male poet idolized and elevated the eroticized lady lover. It can be concluded that libidinal energies run differently, or on different tracks, depending on whether erotic relations are lateral or vertical.

Antithetical to Eroticism

134

Mechanics disrupt the flow of erotic energies. Eroticism is not mechanical; nor does it follow an already written script that follows rigid categorization and classification.

135

On family grounds. Obsession with procreation and child-rearing diminishes the worth of erotic disposition. New types of relations between procreation and eroticism, those that are agonistic and not antagonistic, are needed in order to overcome the trap of dualism between these two human functions and experiences.

136

On medical/hygenics grounds. The scare that is widespread in society about Sexually Transmitted Diseases, whether they are real or not, desensitize the libidinal forces and desexualize human relations.

137

On educational grounds. Parents and children who prevent or retard teenagers' sexual formation often adversely impact their erotic lives.

138

On scientific grounds. What Foucault calls 'scientia sexualis' is an extension of the bookish Alexandrian culture into the field of sexuality. Knowledge, this type of pervasive knowledge, can intrude and interfere with the living experience of sexuality and impoverish it.

139

On religious grounds. Religious conformists retard erotic formation due to their belief in unconditional sexual abstinence.

140

Moralists, prudes, puritans, and those who preach unconditional moderation, that is, moderation at all places and times, are the biggest enemies of 'ars erotica'.

141

Prejudices of all types from racism to ageism hinder authentic human interaction in general and impact and limit erotic relations.

142

The known, the usual, and the familiar, unless the unfamiliar is uncovered in the familiar, make erotic bonds dull and obtund erotic sensitivities.

143

Although voyeurism can be erotically charged for some, it may be a counter-trend in the spirit of eroticism, because the latter assumes active participation while the former is participation from a distance. On the other hand, voyeurism, if integrated into the act in one way or another, may be construed as erotic.

144

Intimacy is sine qua non of eroticism; however, erotic intimacy does not have to be as enduring as it is in romantic love. Intimacy entails reciprocal flow of libido among singular eroticians. What weighs here the most is not equality but rather reciprocity in which the desires of singulars express themselves in the erotic bond, even among total strangers intimacy and strangeness being not antithetical. Equality, namely that all participants must experience erotic pleasures in the same way, goes against erotic culture.

145

Pornography vs. eroticism. Modern pornography, no doubt, is one step forward in sexual exploration; however, it does reflect many of the symptoms of the old regime of repression of sexuality. It is mechanical and categorical/classificatory and, therefore, prescriptive, whereas eroticism is singularly creative, experimental, and open ended. In many ways pornography has permeated into spaces which should be typically occupied by erotic forces.

Eroticism in the Age of Posthumanism

146

Being and becoming are conjoined in the erotic union; there is no separation between the moment and the eternal, as there is no transcendence in the old sense.

147

An erotic culture assumes a non-dualistic approach to mind/body problem, as it embraces embodiment.

148

Saving humanity through technology, an ideal for transhumanism, should not be a goal for posthumanism; what is at stake are values and technology is simply one field of value among many.

149

Anthropocentricism has its roots in ancient humanity; as humans evolved, they felt the necessity to see themselves apart from nature and the animal world from which they came. In later stages, this led to human supremacy and speciesism. In claiming that eroticism belongs strictly to the human realm, a claim made by Bataille, one must not fall into anthropocentricism.

150

Kaleidoscope would be a good metaphor for erotic experiences, as it connotes diversity and perpetual becoming.

How the World of Eros Finally Fell into Oblivion in the West

151

In the Homeric age of archaic Greece the bodily regimes retained their vitality, as the agonistics and erotics reciprocally invigorated each other.

152

In the classical age, the bodily regimes gradually erode, partly due to the rise of ultra-rationalism. The homage made to Eros by the symposiasts with no "entertainment" in *The Symposium* of Plato and in other similar symposia may be a sign of that erosion and decline.

153

The Romans pay tribute to Amor (Eros) who has already lost its vitality by that time; one needs to read Ovid and his sublimated version of love in order to detect this loss.

154

Medievals put Eros to sleep; this is one meaning of Nietzsche's warning that Christianity gave poison to Eros. St. Agustine's

Confessions is one early testimony to what happens to Eros right at the outset of the Middle Ages.

155

In the late phase of the Middle Ages, the troubadours of Occitan make an artistic/poetic experiment to bring Eros back to life, despite medieval constraints.

156

Finally, the Renaissance opens up more gateways for erotic activities and culture; the Reform movement, however, puts a choke hold on it.

World Erotica and the Historic Context

157

From ancient Egypt there is hardly any surviving erotic art or literature, but in one that has survived erotic scenes are depicted with acrobatics and huge male genitalia. If the erotic art were scanty in ancient Egypt, this may be an indication of erotic withdrawal at the onset of human civilization.

158

Unlike the Egyptian and monotheistic trend, ancient China, India and Greece did not suffer from an erotic withdrawal in the civilizing process.

159

In ancient times, it is often claimed that the wealthy, leisurely class could 'afford' erotic activities, as conveyed in ancient Greek, Roman, and Indian literature and art. There is no proof, however, that lower classes, who were not literate or had leisurely time, did not practice erotica. On the other hand, one may go to earlier societies where such class distinctions had not existed yet. One would still find erotic traces, evidence allowing: eroticism is what makes humans distinct from other animal beings and, paradoxically enough, it is also their connection to the animal world.

160

Homage to Parmenides. Erotic activities mend the broken chain of Being.

161

In the late phase of the Middle Ages, the troubadours of Occitan make an artistic/poetic experiment to bring Eros back to life, despite medieval constraints.

162

Finally, the Renaissance opens up more gateways for erotic activities and culture; the Reform movement, however, puts a choke hold on it.

163

The medievals introduced 'morose delectation' into sexuality and instilled a frustrated state of being into the human soul vis-à-vis the object and subject of desire. This is contrary to the seductive element of eroticism, which is open ended and does not have the closure that 'morose delectation' creates.

164

The supremacy and the hegemony of the mind in opposition to the body is a symptom for the decline of all bodily regimes, including sexuality and eroticism.

165

Monetary concerns in and for sex, especially when they are immediately tied to self-preservation, may blunt the erotic drive.

166

The dualism between doing and knowing is overcome in erotic culture.

167

An international alphabet and a universal symbolism of world erotica must be created. Through such alphabet and symbolism, eroticians will be able to "communicate" their desires across cultures and boundaries.

168

Free spirits, unite! Free spirits, wherever they may be on earth, must invest in the creation of an erotic culture; they will, however, be faced with obstacles from a) old society, old repressive moral codes that deny sexuality and its many forms; b) nihilism and its "anything goes" mentality; c) abuses and reactions against the old order; and d) politically correctness of recent times, which deems everyone to fit into one mold and dictates the same type of conduct from everyone, regardless of context.

169

Post-modern and posthumanist critique of humanism and its mind/body dualism is in congruence with eroticism, as it is a holistic experience where mind, body, language, and all that is human melt into one bundle of orgiastic communion.

170

Techne and technology must be driven by eroticism not the other way around. This is one difference between contemporary pornography and eroticism.

171

Robot or machine sex partner is an oxymoron; sex belongs to organic beings and eroticism to humans. What robots do and can do is a different discussion. Let's not obfuscate and diminish the worth of organic life and the human body, lest we fall into "ascetic idealism."

172

Technology must enhance erotic practices, not diminish their quality in mechanics, and meet the sex drive in creative deeds; in other words, the sex drive must manifest itself as *poesis*, as art.

Reflections on the Eroticians of the World

173

Anakreon paid homage to Eros, Dionysus and Aphrodite, gods of sexual life and ecstasy, and the boys and the girls he loved, as he danced and drank wine. The joys of living that are easy to fulfill are the pre-conditions of his eroticism that is difficult to find in everyday life.

174

Arabic eroticians created many different erotic/playful names for sexual organs. How many names does it take to be satisfied? As many as it takes for the wild, erotic imagination. Nefzavi, in his *Parfumed Garden*, lists more than 30 names for both the male and the female organ, where the names designate not only their qualities but also how they appeal to different senses from touch to taste. In addition to these many names, Nefzavi writes on the many positions for sex; however, since the number and the gender of sexual partners are of endless variety, not to mention the many different environments and erotic objects used, sex positions will also be endless. One can benefit from Nefzavi's imagination and expand it manifold with one's own.

175

Bataille connected eroticism to death, which is still hard to understand for the many, since they do not see the ecstatic connection that ties the two. Nor do they see that life and death are one, as the eternal return of the same signifies.

176

Foucault pitched 'ars erotica' against 'scientia sexualis' in his *History of Sexuality*, but both are needed; it is a matter of their prioritization and relation. It is essential for the vitality of a culture not to let the latter be invasive. This is the warning thinkers since Nietzsche have issued; they understand the danger of a culture losing its force and vibrancy when it becomes bookish, a culture of the dry, passive scholar.

177

Homage to St. Genet. It takes courage to turn a prison house into an erotic house.

178

Guilhem IX, Duke of Aquitaine, the first known troubadour of Occitan, used animal symbolism in his erotic verses, especially equestrian symbolism, to honor his lady lovers. In this way, he expressed his respect and gratitude for his horse, a close companion of the knight, and his lovers.

179

Hindu eroticians displayed gods in erotic acts in Varanase, as they conceived their theodicy in this way, keeping a distance to "ascetic idealism" while cultivating their own brand of ascetic practices. Generally speaking, askesis does not and should not exclude erotic practices. Yes, one can speak of "erotic askesis".

180

The Shunga of **Japanese erotica** played different roles and reflected different aspects of eroticism. First, it portrays a variety of erotic themes: positions, dressing vs. nudity, context of sexual encounter, fantasy vs. reality play, body postures and language, different sexual inclinations and preferences, and voyeurism. In some scenes royals join the sex after watching it from a distance. Second, the *shungas* played sex education role as they could be used for sexual practices and arousal. More often than not they served as 'Ersatz' for poor men who could not afford to pay the geishas. On the other hand, shungas were used by lovers as a foreplay so that they could be aroused further.

181

Kama Sutra presents a variety of sexual positions which assume the agility of the body, cultivated in many forms of askesis in Hinduism as in Yoga. This is to say, erotic experiences are enriched when the fitness and mobility of the body are enhanced.

182

Kierkegaard's art of seduction placed an emphasis on sustaining erotic desire without a fulfillment or closure; it is like an open-ended matrix through which the erotic desire can move in a myriad of way.

183

Klossowski's main contribution to world erotica is to show a) how concupiscent simulacra are produced, b) the role of the daemonic in that production, perhaps under the influence of Gide, and c) the significance and relevance of "cult domains" for the formation and expression of erotic desire. To summarize, for Klossowski erotic fantasies are produced as simulacra, as the demon stokes and provokes them in specific contexts or, cult domains.

184

Laure transformed the « sullied sex » of her Catholic upbringing into sacred dirty sex of the new postmodern world order. And for her great liberation was possible beyond all vice and virtue, beyond good and evil.

185

The erotic is ambiguous and elusive as **Lou Salomé** insightfully observes, because it is suspended between the physical and the spiritual and hangs in that void between the singular and the universal. It is precisely because of its complex and paradoxical nature that it is shunned, rejected, and often oppressed by the mainstream.

186

Louÿs said : "there was nothing more sacred than physical love, nothing more beautiful than the human body." Well said to turn the tide of ascetic idealism. Even more sacred, however, is to bring together all forces that make the human back again.

187

The problem that Henry **Miller** faced with his book, Tropic of Cancer, which was condemned by many judges and moralists, is the *eternal* problem of humanity. The homogeneous (of the everyday world) and the heterogeneous (of the "underworld") do not mix, or they do not mix in this way. The heterological must have its own cult domain, protected by its own gods. In the absence of that, the heterogeneous will always be subject to the abuses of the mundane. Ovid had faced a similar problem, centuries before Miller, when his Art of Love became public (and a public scandal). So did many other eroticians of the world. Here is the verdict of a judge on Miller's book: "*Cancer* is not a book. It is a cesspool, an open sewer, a pit of putrefaction, a slimy gathering of all that is rotten in the debris of human depravity." What a *depraved* judgment on an erotic work of art.

188

Nin viewed sex as a holistic experience. To her, sex is not just a mechanical obsession, as it is for Sade, for instance. It rather absorbs the whole human-being, the intellect, the imagination, the emotion and all things that make a human human. And Nin does not separate sex from feelings, from the love of the whole human-being, which she considers to be her feminine point, an expression of her feminine self. All of what Nin says, however, does not go against promiscuity: a sex encounter may be short and yet still be holistic, as feeling and sex are conjoined.

189

Through the Greco-Roman web of myth, **Ovid** masterfully weaves the broken threads of play between poetry and erotica, as he exposes the rules of the game of the "bedroom".

190

Plato coined the term 'erotike' in *The Symposium*. Contemporary eroticism, however, has deviated from it and variegated, as it has embraced all genders and singular orientations and emphasized lateral erotic relations. Nonetheless, the lofty and sublime heights Plato set for erotic education remains and should remain.

191

Quietude can serve eroticism as it contributes to the formation of the self.

192

Sade is a ground-breaker in the art of erotica in the west, although his pornographic novels portray sexual acts in a mechanical way and sexual violence remains not transfigured to a large extent. Regarding the first points, eroticism does not follow a mechanical or a methodic order of things. As for the second, eroticism does not exclude violence per se; it is rather channeled and projected unto higher realms of interaction where all participants find their higher fulfilled selves. In Sade, on the other hand, there is a Manichean division of types where those who are not deemed libertine can be violated any time by any libertine.

193

Sappho's great achievement, in addition to her poetry, lies in creating small islands for free-spirited women in the bigger society of patriarchy and tyranny in her country, Lesbos. In those islands women could celebrate their erotic and artistic selves.

194

Taoist eroticians focused on preserving the libidinal energies so as to sustain the erotic process for longer durations of time, analogous to Kierkegaard's emphasis on seduction in eroticism. This sustenance of erotic sex can be achieved by the Taoist method, *wu wei wu*, act but do not act, push and pull, insert and withdraw.

195

Zeno's philosophy, also called Stoicism, calls for strength in all things that happen and could happen to humans and must be lauded in that regard. However, it creates closures for human emotions and desires and their expressions, which are antithetical to erotic experience. Moreover, like many other Socratic and post-Socratic schools it upholds moderation in all contexts of human relations. Eroticism, however, is nothing but moderate.

Epilogue

196

Rediscovery of eroticism will heal the soul, modulate emotions, and bring together the broken pieces of human life.

197

In his critique of Western discourse on and attitude to sexuality, and consequently sexual practices (although this is not the main focus of the book), Foucault calls for the cultivation of 'ars erotica' — the seas are open and the skies are high — let's embark!

197

At this stage of decline in "ars erotica," all fields of human interest must work together in order to recover it. New spiritual formations will carve out fields for it and introduce a plethora of rituals and initiation rites. Arts will show how sexuality can be experienced in many creative ways. Philosophy will reflect on the body, its primacy, and power. Sciences have furnished, as there are many studies, and will furnish further a body of knowledge on human sexuality. Psychology and psychoanalysis have emphasized the importance of healthy sexual life for a healthy soul. Linguistics will help discover an erotic language, with the hope of sidestepping linguistic debasement of sexuality and gender biases.

A Mini-Bibliography of World Erotica

Anacreon — Greek Lyric II, translated by D. A. Campbell, Loeb Classical Library, Harvard University Press, 1988.

Bataille, G. — Erotism, translated by M. Dalwood, City Light Books, 1986

Foucault, M. — History of Sexuality, Vol. 1, translated by R. Hurley, Vintage, 1980.

Fowkes, C. (editor) — The Illustrated Kama Sutra, Ananga-Ranga • Perfumed Garden, translated by Sir Richard Burton & F. F. Arbuthnot, Park Street Press, 1991.

Freud, S. — Basic Writings of Sigmund Freud, translated by Dr. A. Brill, The Modern Library, 1938.

Horunobu/Koryusai — Japanese erotic prints, Hotei Publishing, 2001.

Klossowski. P. — Diana at her Bath and The Women of Rome, translated by S. Hawkes and S. Sartarelli, Marsilio, 1990.

Laure	Laure : The Collected Writings, translated by Jeanine Herman, City Light Books, 1995.
Salome-Andreas, L.	The Erotic, translated by J. Crisp, Routledge, 2013.
Louÿs, P.	The She Devils, translated by John Phillips, Creation Books, 1998.
Miller, H.	Tropic of Cancer, Grove, 2007.
Moravia, A.	Erotic Tales, translated by Tim Parks, Farrar, Straus & Giroux, 1985.
Nafzavi	Perfumed Garden, translated by R. F. Burton, Blueberry Books, 2016.
Nelli, R.	L'érotique des Troubadours, Toulouse, 1984.
Néret. G.	Erotica Universalis, Taschen, 2005.
Nietzsche, F.	The Birth of Tragedy, translated by W. Kaufmann, Vintage Books, 1967.
Nin, A.	Delta of Venus, Mariner, 2004.

Ovid	The Art of Love, translated by James Michie, The Modern Library, 2002.
Plato	The Symposium, translated by A. Nehamas & P. Woodruff, Hackett, 1989.
Réage, P.	Story of O, translated by John Paul Hand, Blue Moon Books, 1993.
Sade, Marquis de	Philosophy in the Bedroom, translated by R. Seaver & A. Wainhouse, Grove, 2007.
Sappho	If Not, Winter: Fragments of Sappho, translated by A. Carson, Vintage, 2003.
von Sacher-Masoch, L.	Venus in Furs, Penguin, 2000.